SPORTS BIOGRAPHIES
JOSÉ ALTUVE

KENNY ABDO

Bolt!
An Imprint of Abdo Zoom
abdopublishing.com

abdopublishing.com

Published by Abdo Zoom, a division of ABDO, P.O. Box 398166, Minneapolis, Minnesota 55439. Copyright © 2019 by Abdo Consulting Group, Inc. International copyrights reserved in all countries. No part of this book may be reproduced in any form without written permission from the publisher. Bolt!™ is a trademark and logo of Abdo Zoom.

Printed in the United States of America, North Mankato, Minnesota.
052018
092018

THIS BOOK CONTAINS RECYCLED MATERIALS

Photo Credits: Alamy, AP Images, Getty Images, Icon Sportswire, iStock
Production Contributors: Kenny Abdo, Jennie Forsberg, Grace Hansen
Design Contributors: Dorothy Toth, Neil Klinepier

Library of Congress Control Number: 2017960657

Publisher's Cataloging-in-Publication Data

Names: Abdo, Kenny, author.
Title: José Altuve / by Kenny Abdo.
Description: Minneapolis, Minnesota : Abdo Zoom, 2019. | Series: Sports biographies |
    Includes online resources and index.
Identifiers: ISBN 9781532124792 (lib.bdg.) | ISBN 9781532124938 (ebook) |
    ISBN 9781532125003 (Read-to-me ebook)
Subjects: LCSH: Altuve, José, -- 1990-, Biography--Juvenile literature. |
    Baseball players--United States—Biography--Juvenile literature. |
    Outfielders (Baseball)--Biography--Juvenile literature. |
    Houston Astros (Baseball team)--Biography--Juvenile literature.
Classification: DDC 796.35709 [B]--dc23

TABLE OF CONTENTS

JOSÉ ALTUVE

José Altuve is short in stature but huge in talent. He plays second base for the Houston Astros.

At 5ft 6in (1.7m), Altuve is the shortest active player in the MLB. He has at least 200 hits recorded each season and has won three batting **championships**.

EARLY YEARS

Altuve was born in Maracay, Venezuela in 1990.

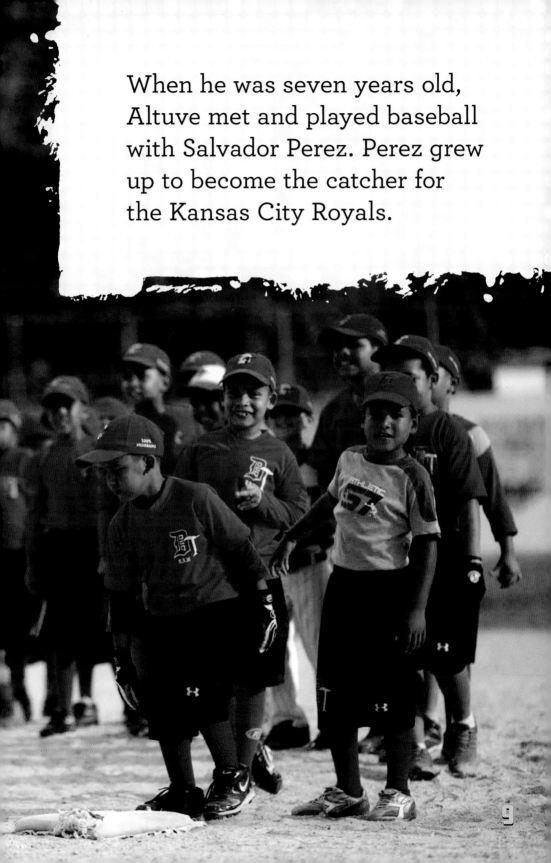

When he was seven years old, Altuve met and played baseball with Salvador Perez. Perez grew up to become the catcher for the Kansas City Royals.

Altuve tried out for the Houston Astros at the age of 17. He was not considered because of his height.

GOING PRO

Altuve continued to work hard. Eventually he impressed the **scouts** enough to get a contract in 2007. He moved to the United States in 2008.

After working his way through the Astros **farm team**, Altuve made his MLB **debut** in July 2011. He made the All-Star team the very next season.

15

In the 2014 season, Altuve became the first player in 80 years to have 130 hits and 40 stolen bases all before the **All-Star Game**.

By the end of the season, he was the first Astro to win a batting **title**. His 225 hits were the most a player had hit within a season in five years.

LEGACY

Altuve became the 9th ballplayer in MLB history to hit three home runs in a single playoff game.

When he's not on the field, Altuve spends time with his wife and daughter, who was born in 2016.

GLOSSARY

All-Star Game – a yearly game played by the best players from the American League (AL) and National League (NL).

championship – a game held to find a first-place winner.

debut – a first appearance.

farm team – a minor league team under the control of the MLB.

scout – a person who watches athletes play to see if they are ready to go professional.

title – a first-place position in a contest.

ONLINE RESOURCES

Booklinks
NONFICTION NETWORK
FREE! ONLINE NONFICTION RESOURCES

To learn more about José Altuve, please visit **abdobooklinks.com**. These links are routinely monitored and updated to provide the most current information available.

INDEX